Masterpieces: Artists and Their Works

Leonardo da Vinci

by Barbara Witteman

Consultant:
Joan Lingen, Ph.D.
Professor of Art History
Clarke College
Dubuque, Iowa

Bridgestone Books
an imprint of Capstone Press
Mankato, Minnesota

Bridgestone Books are published by Capstone Press
1710 Roe Crest Drive, North Mankato, Minnesota 56003.
www.capstonepub.com

Library of Congress Cataloging-in-Publication Data
Witteman, Barbara.
    Leonardo da Vinci / by Barbara Witteman.
    p. cm.—(Masterpieces: artists and their works)
    Summary: Discusses the life, works, and lasting influence of Leonardo da Vinci.
    Includes bibliographical references and index.
    13-digit: 978-0-7368-2228-2 (library binding)
    10-digit: 0-7368-2228-3 (library binding)
    13-digit: 978-0-7368-3407-0 (softcover pbk.)
    10-digit: 0-7368-3407-9 (softcover pbk.)
    1. Leonardo, da Vinci, 1452–1519—Juvenile literature. 2. Artists—Italy—Biography—
Juvenile literature. [1. Leonardo, da Vinci, 1452–1519. 2. Artists. 3. Scientists. 4. Painting,
Italian.] I. Title. II. Series.
N6923.L33 W57 2004
709'.2—dc21   2003000063

Editorial Credits
Blake Hoena, editor; Heather Kindseth, series designer; Juliette Peters, book designer;
    Alta Schaffer, photo researcher; Karen Risch, product planning editor

Photo Credits
Art Resource, NY, 16; Réunion Des Musées Nationaux, cover (left), 20 ; Scala, cover (right),
    4, 8 10 (both), 12; Erich Lessing, 6, 18
Corbis/Bettmann, 14

Printed in the United States of America in North Mankato, Minnesota.
042013
007264R

Table of Contents

In *Lady with an Ermine,* shading shows the details of the
weasel's white fur. Leonardo was one of the first painters
to use shadows to make his paintings look more lifelike.

Leonardo da Vinci

Leonardo da Vinci (1452–1519) lived during the Renaissance. This period of European history lasted from the early 1300s to the late 1500s. It was a time of new learning. Artists worked with new art styles. Scientists studied nature. Explorers found new lands. The Renaissance was a good time for Leonardo to be alive. He was an artist, an inventor, and a scientist.

Even though he had many talents, Leonardo had one big weakness. He left most of his work unfinished. He only completed a few paintings. He often started a painting, got a new idea, and then began a new project.

Some of Leonardo's ideas were inventions. He drew pictures of diving suits and weapons. He even hoped to build a flying machine.

Leonardo was also a scientist. He studied the bodies of animals and people. He learned how many parts of the human body work.

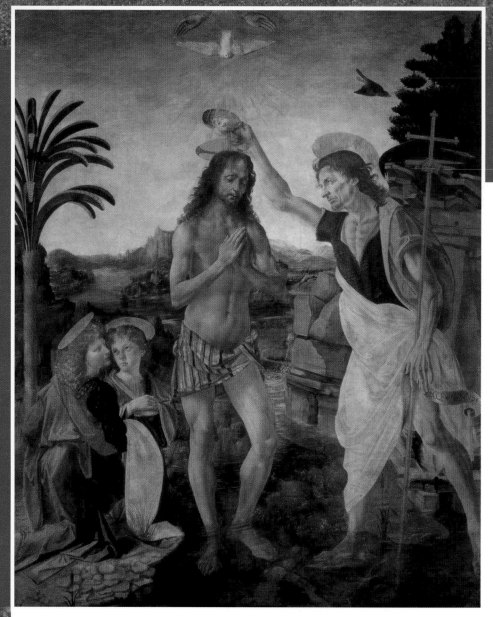

Leonardo painted the angel on the far left in Verrochio's painting *Baptism of Christ*. Apprentices often worked on their teachers' paintings.

Young Leonardo

Leonardo was born April 15, 1452, in Vinci, Italy. His mother, Caterina, was a poor farmer. His father, Ser Piero, was a rich lawyer. Leonardo's parents did not marry. He grew up with his father's family.

During the 1400s, children of unmarried parents were not allowed to go to a university. Leonardo could not study to be a lawyer like his father. He could not study to be a banker or a doctor. He had to learn a different type of job.

Leonardo liked to draw. Ser Piero showed his son's drawings to Andrea del Verrochio. Verrochio was a famous artist living in Florence, Italy. He liked Leonardo's drawings. In 1466, Leonardo became Verrochio's apprentice. Verrochio taught Leonardo to draw, paint, sculpt, and design buildings.

In *Adoration of the Magi*, Leonardo made the people and animals look as if they were moving. He was one of the first Renaissance artists to try and show motion in his work.

Adoration of the Magi

Leonardo's skills as a painter earned him work. In 1481, he was hired to paint *Adoration of the Magi* for San Donato at Scopeto. This church was near Florence. Leonardo's painting shows the three wise men coming to see Jesus Christ.

During Leonardo's lifetime, artists drew a full-sized sketch of the picture they would paint. This drawing was called a cartoon. Artists attached the cartoon to the painting's surface. They then traced the drawing on the surface. Next, artists created the underpainting. They shaded the painting with brown and gray colors. Lastly, artists added the other colors to their work.

It took Leonardo more than one year to finish the cartoon and underpainting for *Adoration of the Magi*. By this time, he was ready to begin a new project. In 1482, Leonardo moved to Milan, Italy. He went to Milan to work for the rich Duke Lodovico Sforza. Leonardo left *Adoration of the Magi* unfinished.

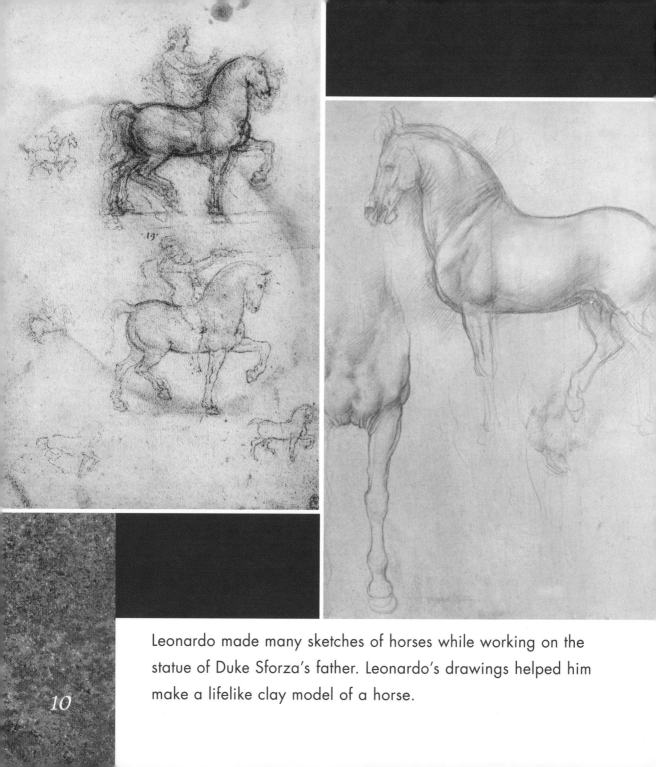

Leonardo made many sketches of horses while working on the statue of Duke Sforza's father. Leonardo's drawings helped him make a lifelike clay model of a horse.

Leonardo's Horse

Renaissance artists created weapons, buildings, and art. Leonardo told Duke Sforza about cannons he could make and canals he could build. Leonardo also offered to make a statue to honor the duke's father.

In 1483, Leonardo began work on the statue. He wanted to show the duke's father riding a horse. First, Leonardo planned to make the horse. It would stand 24 feet (7.3 meters) tall and be the world's tallest statue of a horse.

Leonardo took years to plan the statue. By 1493, he finished a full-sized clay model of the horse. He also had gathered 29 tons (26 metric tons) of tin and copper. He would make the finished statue with these metals.

Sadly, Leonardo was not able to complete his work. In 1499, the French army attacked Milan. The metal Leonardo had collected was used to make cannon balls. Archers shot arrows at the clay horse for target practice.

In the *Last Supper,* Judas (fourth figure from the left) clutches a purse in his right hand. The purse holds the money he was given to betray Jesus (center).

The Last Supper

In Milan, Leonardo worked on many projects. He began a painting in Santa Maria delle Grazie in 1495. He painted the *Last Supper* on the dining room wall of this building.

Leonardo painted a dramatic scene in the *Last Supper*. It shows the Apostles' reactions after Jesus Christ tells them that he will be killed. Some of Jesus' followers motion with their hands. Others lean toward Jesus. These actions help show how the Apostles' felt about Jesus' news.

Leonardo used perspective in the *Last Supper*. This art method was new to Renaissance artists. Perspective shows depth and distance in a painting. In the *Last Supper,* the picture looks like it goes back into a room.

In Milan, Leonardo also worked on inventions. He made a bright lamp to read by at night. Leonard built a plumbing system for the duke's castle. He designed a diving suit, a helicopter, and a tank. Hundreds of years later, people would use his ideas to build these machines.

Leonardo drew body parts like the heart, but his drawings were not used by Renaissance doctors. They thought people should read books to learn about the body instead of looking at pictures.

Anatomy Studies

Artists often study the human body. They learn about anatomy so they can make lifelike paintings and statues of people. During Leonardo's time, artists would go to hospitals or morgues to study dead bodies. They cut open the bodies to study their muscles and bones.

Leonardo also wanted to know how the body worked. He cut open bodies and drew sketches of their parts. He learned that nerves begin in the spinal cord. He saw that the heart had chambers. He made drawings of the brain and the skeleton. Leonardo knew more about the human body than most scientists of his time.

Leonardo often studied the heart. He made a glass model of the aorta. The aorta carries blood away from the heart. Leonardo attached his model to a cow's heart filled with water. With his model, Leonardo learned that valves in the heart open and close. Valves control the flow of blood between the heart's chambers.

Leonardo designed a parachute (left center). He said a person could use it to jump from great heights without getting hurt. He also made notes about his ideas for a flying machine.

Leonardo's Notes

Leonardo had an unusual way of writing. He wrote his notes from right to left. The notes could be read by holding them up to a mirror. Historians think Leonardo wrote this way because he was left handed. Writing from right to left kept his hand from smearing ink as he wrote.

Leonardo wrote more than 5,000 pages of notes. He made notes about his ideas for inventions. He wrote down what he learned about the human body. Leonardo also took notes about the things he saw while walking.

Leonardo pasted some of his notes into books. Others were left as he wrote them. Most of Leonardo's notes have been lost. Only about one-third of them have been found. In 1965, two of Leonardo's notebooks were found in a library in Spain.

Today, ten of Leonardo's notebooks are known to exist. They are in museums and libraries in England, Italy, France, and Spain. One notebook is in a private collection in the United States.

With *Mona Lisa,* Leonardo achieved something very unusual.
No matter where people stand to look at this painting, they
feel that *Mona Lisa* is staring back at them.

Mona Lisa

In 1506, Leonardo finished his most famous painting, *Mona Lisa*. He tried something new with this painting. He blurred the outlines of objects in the background, making them look unreal. *Mona Lisa* was one of Leonardo's favorite paintings. He kept it with him for the rest of his life.

In 1516, King Francis I of France offered Leonardo a job. Leonardo moved to the king's home in Amboise. He served as the First Painter, Architect, and Mechanic to the King. Mostly, he and Francis talked about Leonardo's ideas and the things he had learned.

On May 2, 1519, Leonardo died. He was 67. Leonardo was buried at the church of Saint Florentine in Amboise. Years later, the church was torn down. Rocks, headstones, and coffins from the cemetery were used to rebuild the church. Today, no one knows if Leonardo's bones are actually in the grave marked with his name.

Virgin of the Rocks shows the Virgin Mary (center) introducing John the Baptist (left) to her son, Jesus (bottom right). Leonardo painted it for the church of San Francesco Grande in Milan.

Leonardo's Fame

For nearly 300 years, Leonardo was known only as an artist. But his few finished paintings changed the way people painted. He used shading and showed movement in his art. He also used perspective to show depth in his paintings. These ideas were new to Renaissance artists.

In the 1800s, people began to look at Leonardo's notes. Historians learned that Leonardo's studies were very advanced. He knew more about the human body than most scientists of his time.

Leonardo's notes also showed drawings of his many ideas. They included plans for diving suits, flying machines, and weapons. There seemed to be no limit to Leonardo's ideas.

Today, Leonardo is remembered for his art as well as his ideas and studies of the body. His art can be seen in museums in France and Italy. His dreams of flying machines and diving suits have come true.

Important Dates

1452—Leonardo da Vinci is born April 15 in Vinci, Italy.

1466—Andrea del Verrochio makes Leonardo his apprentice.

1470—Verrochio begins to paint *Baptism of Christ*; Leonardo paints the angel on the far left side of this painting.

1481—The church of San Donato at Scopeto hires Leonardo to paint *Adoration of the Magi.*

1482—Leonardo moves to Milan, Italy, to work for Duke Lodovico Sforza.

1483—Leonardo begins to paint *Lady with an Ermine.*

1489—Leonardo begins his studies of anatomy.

1492—Christopher Columbus discovers the Americas.

1495—Leonardo begins to paint the *Last Supper.*

1499—The French army captures Milan.

1503—Leonardo begins to paint *Mona Lisa.*

1506—Leonardo begins to paint *Virgin of the Rocks.*

1508—Leonardo begins to paint *Virgin and Child with Saint Anne* (shown on cover).

1516—King Francis I invites Leonardo to move to France.

1519—Leonardo dies in Amboise, France, on May 2.

Words to Know

anatomy (uh-NAT-uh-mee)—the study of the human body
Apostle (uh-POSS-uhl)—one of Jesus Christ's 12 followers
apprentice (uh-PREN-tiss)—someone who learns a trade or craft by working with a skilled person
architect (AR-ki-tekt)—a person who designs buildings
betray (bi-TRAY)—to do something that is not loyal
canal (kuh-NAL)—a channel that ships can use to sail between bodies of water
chamber (CHAYM-bur)—a space in the heart that holds blood
morgue (MORG)—a place where dead bodies are kept
perspective (pur-SPEK-tiv)—depth in a painting; perspective shows distant objects being smaller than nearer ones.
Renaissance (REN-uh-sahnss)—a time of new art and learning
sketch (SKECH)—a rough drawing
valve (VALV)—a movable part that controls the flow of liquid

Read More

Connolly, Sean. *Leonardo da Vinci.* The Life and Work of. Des Plaines, Ill.: Heinemann Library, 2000.
Fritz, Jean. *Leonardo's Horse.* New York: Putnam, 2001.

Useful Addresses

Boston Museum of Science
Science Park
Boston, MA 02114

National Gallery of Art
2000B South Club Drive
Landover, MD 20785

Internet Sites

Do you want to find out more about Leonardo da Vinci?
Let FactHound, our fact-finding hound dog,
do the research for you.

Here's how:
1) Visit *http://www.facthound.com*.
2) Type in the **BOOK ID** number: **0736822283**.
3) Click on **FETCH IT**.

FactHound will fetch Internet sites picked by our editors just for y

Index